SYL CHENEY-COKER was bo[...] and educated at the Universit[...] in the USA. He has held univer[...] ments and was a visiting writer [...] Program at the University of Iowa in 1988. He is the author of two previous volumes of poetry and the novel *The Last Harmattan of Alusine Dunbar* (Heinemann African Writers Series, 1990).

SYL CHENEY-COKER

THE BLOOD IN THE DESERT'S EYES

POEMS

HEINEMANN

Heinemann International
a division of Heinemann Educational Books Ltd
Halley Court, Jordan Hill, Oxford OX2 8EJ

Heinemann Educational Books Inc
361 Hanover Street, Portsmouth, New Hampshire, 03801, USA

Heinemann Educational Books (Nigeria) Ltd
PMB 5205, Ibadan
Heinemann Kenya Ltd
Kijabe Street, PO Box 45314, Nairobi
Heinemann Educational Boleswa
PO Box 10103, Village Post Office, Gaborone, Botswana
Heinemann Publishers (Caribbean) Ltd
175 Mountain View Avenue, Kingston 6, Jamaica

LONDON EDINBURGH MELBOURNE SYDNEY
AUCKLAND SINGAPORE HARARE
MADRID ATHENS BOLOGNA

© Syl Cheney-Coker 1990
First published by Heinemann International
in the African Writers Series in 1990

Illustrated by Vinston Bair

British Library Cataloguing in Publication Data
Cheney-Coker, Syl
The Blood in The Desert's Eyes. – (Heinemann African poets).
I. Title II. Series
821

ISBN 0–435–90574–0

Phototypeset by Wilmaset, Birkenhead, Wirral
Printed in Great Britain by
Cox and Wyman, Reading, Berkshire

90 91 92 93 94 95 10 9 8 7 6 5 4 3 2 1

CONTENTS

Apocalypse 1
The Outsider 3
The Philosopher 4
The Blood in the Desert's Eyes 5
Cactus Needles 6
Sophistry 9
The Diaspora 10
Cotillion 12
The Painting 14
Season 17
Bird Song 18
Caliban 19
Pilgrim 20
Sonata and Rain 22
Illumination 25
Bread 26
The Baptism of the Orphan 28
To a Dead Poet 30
The Brotherhood of Man 32
The Gambler 33
The Afternoon of Your Diamond 34
Children of Amnesty 36
The Night of the Beasts 38
Prisoner of Conscience 39
They Shot the Poet Once 40
The Refugee 41
The Children of Palestine 42
Aftermath 44
The Tin Gods 45
The Zealots 46
Exodus 49
Song on a Chinese Flute 50

The Masquerade 53
Stone 54
Solstice 55
Logos 56
Rite of Passage 59
Song 60
The Soldier 62
The Artist 63
Childhood 64
The Muse 65
Anniversary 67
The Sun 68
Portrait 69
Night Whistle 70
Mask 71
The Miracle of the Morning 72
The Walk of the Blind 73
Desire 75
Dead Eyes 76
The Plague 78
Children of Adam 80
This Side of Humanity 82
End of the Game 84

'For Man cannot unite with Man but by their Emanations
Which stand both Male & Female at the Gates of each
   Humanity
How then can I ever again be united as Man with Man
While thou, my Emanation, refusest my Fibres of
   Dominion?
When Souls mingle and join thro'all the Fibres of
   Brotherhood
Can there be any secret joy on Earth greater than this?'

      Jerusalem, Chapter Four by William Blake.

THE POEMS

Apocalypse

In the country where I was born,
where I shall succumb to my infinite number,
feel my disjointed bones, I know
that the cup of life is a huge brain
that will descend to our knees!
A cup of life: like the cries of labour
heard in those white rooms composed of women
those valleys of entrepreneurial vultures
where delirious from want, the lepers enunciate
their combustible chests with a prodigious absence of
   fingers!

Standing between palisades they speak their putative verbs
that go riding the hunchbacks who do not conform to
   beauty
with their ancient, archeological way of walking
they fall off the lips of the waifs, skeletal beggars
scratching their soup bowls, seated at his right hand,
these thieves of the sepulchre I call my brothers

confluence of hands over the unleavened bread,
his table invites your procession in hunger
labourer, student, the miners who cough coming from their
   shift:
exposed animals without masks to keep their hearts from
   dying;
they come on their knees summoned in mid-life, they
   declaim
their earnings in pustules, portraying their elements,

these ferocious cannibals at his table!
Ah, to lift them up to the thrice-tempted Christ
going from their source to wilderness
without cane or camel, diurnal pillory of the father;
Antonio Vivaldi the red priest plays for you
wild echoes in the desert where walking in solitude and
　　hope
he prepares your conclave, Hieronymous, the lone traveller

so drinking your alkaline syrup at night
you watch those paralytic children in your shacks
surprised that they cough so much,
stretched out, adumbrated and confused like extinct apes,
those soporific children of your loins;
lost in your soup bowl you feed them with your last eggs
preserved from gryphon, these brains that will descend to
　　your knees,
you name them Christ between two tears opposed to crying
and finally embrace them, these children opposed to
　　children.

The Outsider

Armed with his crutches, the thief, wolf-like,
steals from the tree; crucify him for that,
or the woman forsaking her child to kiss
the angelic feet of Mary Magdalene; stone her for that

observe the cripples painted by Bruegel
skinning the corpse of a dog; call out
the sanitary van for that, or the crazed
desecrating the dowager's gown; cauterize him for that

draining his glass of resin the neophyte prays
before a God supine, he prays before a resonant stone
two-headed existence, the godhead bad, the godhead good
thinking how they have released him but not his soul

alone, his soul comes seeking that which was stolen
from him, the pilgrim's path to faith, his soul
is a crown of thorns, the girl with the harelip
is his soul destroyed, that man at the foot of Golgotha
lonely beginning lonely redemption

lifting his chain O Lord, give him the text
of your annunciation! for who would dine released
from your cross when the pastoral is lost?

in the hour of your trial Lord
deliver from your cross your brother Barabbas!

The Philosopher

Who lived here when the stones were green
verdigris of age when the reptiles
marched like men into the night
before that morning the sea emptying
its cup of wounds like a chasm of revolt?
like a castaway an old man kept his books in a cave
desolate his memory of life a portrait
like an abstraction of years, he lived
forgotten by others before the last tidal wave
I consecrate him seer his beard was a white book
where we read about prophets and kings
planners of the ruins astride our stormy conscience
to write what history the moon
already dripping its sea of red blood

the whirlwind that licked over your body
amulet of season playing fangs on the translucent word
flagellant you lived at crossroads where the word was nailed
neologist who dressed the world in hendecasyllabic verse
O monk saddened when you consecrated the word in body
stripped when you meditated in penury

you return shadow from shadow the word
transformed into phoenix you return the man
reigning the length of the raised cross
amidst the pus the world opens unto tomorrow
violated your soul we fashion you in memory
drift of a cyclone, man with whom we raise our conscience
you rise from your body to be equal to your name!

The Blood in the Desert's Eyes

Smoking their laudanum of life the men
came up to earth bearing their universal ash
the black bread of life kneaded on their brows
they crawled like those Methusalahan turtles
that grow melancholy with age
undulated neighing of their jackasses the ulcerative
longing to eat expressed in their cheekbones
brooding, contrary to their peaceful glow, being that
they display those enlarged proboscises
flexing the want of which I write

the breasts of two perfect moons fashioned like Cyclops
enormous ray of sunlight showing the point
at which the animal in man triumphs over these men
seizing them in their centrifugal rage
advanced dementia of reason, the thoracic longing
that kills rib to rib the archetypal mother
clutching her belly!

let us be done with the desire to be a father
before the son, the want that takes the child
from birth to death; praise to the stoic, the cripple
who breaks his bread with me, seeing upside down
his world, and going back from earth enormous with rage
the men keep time with the mocking grandfather sun
showing the blood in the desert's eyes!

Cactus Needles

*'I am the man,
I suffered,
I was there.'*

Walt Whitman

Strikers of Sierra Leone
guided by your darkness when they put out the light
the yokes of your shoulders, your mirrors that reflect
your docility that kills with tenderness
strikers when the streets give birth to teargas
the jails to children the hospital to the wounded
your pedestrian sagacity that speaks without polishing
your words, without the aromatic lies, the napes
of your necks gleaming with the vehemence waiting
to be born; for you the chimeric books quote
their puerile laws, the gun its smoke
the gallows its rope, the brute its strength
the mortuary its linen of red blood
and the cemetery its prodigious appetite
to love wholeheartedly your vegetable hearts!

Workers of the bronchial, the tubercular
siphoning your petrol from the granite
without rancour without the hate that is born of hate
workers shoeing your soles with your carapace
before marching toward their paltry years
before they counted the dead of the street
the dead of the woman the dead of the child
sucking and then dying on the dried-out teat

professors of my country closing your books
professors of symmetry of the logic of all logics
snivelling before the avuncular, the otiose
the gunpowder was singing, I tell you, seeing them suffer
cooking the rice that grew from its grain of sawdust
the tomato its paste of vampire blood, I know
lawyers of my country eyeing your diamonds
your parliamentary seats opposing their votes
these workers belying the calm of the sea
the grandiloquent tapestry of Sierra Leone!

Ferule of the rustic bread whipping below the stomach
cannons of the dregs, these cactus growths at the summit
of their hunger, telling me with garlic sweat with poison gas
O granulated dreams! O threadbare future!
O toxic feast of the master
Nero amidst the lean spewing his potassium vomit!
Meanwhile workers of Sierra Leone proceeding to your
    analysis
the true beginning of every joy measured by the mistrial
proceeding in alphabet without the captive noun
dolorous brothers of the order of the pascal lamb
the passover will come, the night that widens the fjord
until then, you suffer, you march you wait
I see, witness of your souls holding the horn of your
    unicorn.

Sophistry

Sombre within the dark I enter my world
listening to the cruel claptrap of its men
their apocryphal laws, disregarding the judges,
so skilfully written, so cleverly quoted
to ennoble the god pushing down our heads

but through the passage of time, how often
have I, weary of the silence of this place, chewing
on the *cola nut*[1] of my rage, sought the cause of this plague
O Jeremiah! O *Bai Bureh*[2]! the hero having fallen asleep?
for all along his paths crisscrossing my land
silver-back of snakes, hyena-sweet of tongue
are men outsmarting the Greeks in the art of sophistry

so beware my country of what is hidden inside their togas
of the cries of 'son of the soil' so meekly uttered
the look of innocence while the caravan crawls through
   your streets
beware of men bearing gifts from gods whose names they
   mis-spell
for the goat's head smells differently from the sheep's
but when the beseecher becomes the executioner
he wields his scimitar equally among the animals.

---

[1]*cola nut* Brownish seed, about the size of a chestnut, produced by a sterculiaceous tree, and common throughout West Africa. When chewed it is said, especially by Moslems, to relieve hunger pains.
[2]*Bai Bureh* Late nineteenth-century Sierra Leonean patriot who fought the British during the so-called 'Hut Tax' War; was captured and sent into exile on the Gold Coast, now Ghana.

The Diaspora

for Freddie and Olivia Jones

In the pallid eyes of an evening
our world transforms itself crawling on its knees
to its beggar's role; it loses its shame, taciturn world
the disgraced half of a world no longer ours
speaking its history in tatters of tears;
it is dying of *kwashiokor*[1], the starved face
of an evening when even the earth itself
already scorched onto the monkey's ass, already counting
in burnt brambles the seasons without rain
has the sad look of the Medusa

and because of this dearth of rain on our land
because of this thirst which sends the monkey to the pepper
   bush
this vigil we keep over the corpse of a land, Sierra Leone
which endlessly produced for others the ripe fruit of the
   earth,
because we are no more what we used to be, the first son
of the sons, the sheep seek shelter in the cellar
where the goats are constipated devouring truth:
truth which is imprisoned in the tissues of our dying world
truth is a skeleton we make a coffin for, the dog
of this life whose ribs they sell to their diviner
the pestiferous hand of night which rapes the reluctant body
of a girl the sole provider in a household of nine
truth is an abandoned mistress!

miserable exiles we sleep on strange beds
but who will call us back, pirate wind, to our world
drifting like deadwood on this nightmarish dance, this
   insanity?
Ah! to make once again our bed of laurels
to hear once more the sound of the feet of men
marching among the minions, the pulsating heart
of this world we must rescue from the dragons
we die no more but tear from our hearts
the stigma of being mute of being cowards!

---

[1] *kwashiokor*   a nutritional disease in infants and children due to a lack of protein (of Ghanaian origin).

Cotillion

And now that they understand, listening,
how men are born, live, father the storm
now that we are no more innocent of the whirlwind
of words cyclic posturing of the *baobab*[1]
we ride the constellations drifters upon seven seas
provoke those ceremonies called to function
spelling out our treason in monotonous syllogism

civic women you lead their cotillion
but the twenty yards of your gowns
are dragged through the violent zero of riot
mopping up the blood reeking of rape

but rancid among their gold more pronounced
than the marvellous denial of their rich
while they break the poor in fours
break them in atrophied ducts drawing with a knife
their profiles but never letting them be
their gold of life their poor of eternity!

let them be for once in front of the mayoral dish
coming to his goblet from their skeletons
musing how having been born weak having
been made men under their *dolmen*² at day
they face the night immense expression of derelict
treading on the hard stones of your conscience!

---

¹*baobab*   Very large tree found all over West Africa, but mostly in Sahel region. Produces a delicious, gourd-like fruit favoured by monkeys.
²*dolmen*   A structure usually regarded as a tomb, consisting of two or more upright stones set with a space between and capped by a horizontal stone.

The Painting

When the undertaker had measured the corpse
he made a coffin fit for the body of a dwarf
when the peninsula woke up one morning
it received a gift in the form of a massacre
when the vultures arrived drawn to the country
by the news of the drought they found
Saturn devouring his children

Goya you painted a country destroying itself
the absolute horror the cannibal instinct
you painted Spain and the agony in the crude heart
of war the agony that destroys the agony that walks
with the gait of an ass that has the morose face
of this baboon of a morning recovering from
the recumbent blow of a storm at dawn when the survivors
timidly put on their shoes pick their teeth
and this dwarf of a day lies flat while the desert
breathes its hot air on the blistering backs of our fatigue!

The rich undertaker looks meanly
at the corpse of the dwarf, the corpse
has a peaceful look the corpse is smiling
this corpse wants no eulogy it wants no funereal song
it scorns remembrances it wants no tomb
but if they put it in a pauper's grave
this corpse will rise, and walking across the cemetery
will strangle the rich man in his grave;
for this corpse is my country!

Goya you painted the heart of Spain
what a pity you are not around to paint my country
    — my heart!

Season

The animal rears its dust
its qualitative form of speech
working its clouds distant from its dreams:
harshness, the ripe-blood pomegranate, enraging the beasts;
thus I exist, functioning in my teacup
bleeding from octopus wound
bleeding from strangulated voice
from their two-penny benediction
forcing me to drink this poisonous brew
to drink this hurt navigating my soul!

living under these clouds
searching for logos, the word
ascends the brain alternating
with my nightmares growing from carrion beginnings
and death spreads its pontificated cloth
weaving that treacherous September
arched over the children's mouths
speaking from naked wounds, O high velocity of mothers!

come with me, do not die yet
removing your skins to make your shrouds
tomorrow will come inspired by the millennium
already functionary marionettes parade in showdragons
perfumed imagery of slough riding the caudal dance
the song of Lilliputians, men that I observe
sailing from country to country holding life
from dying in the season of living good.

Bird Song

The powder with which I'll cure myself
meditating on life, on the migraine
before meditating on sixpence has arrived
now that seeing the powder the bird
wants its own sixpence, meditating on feathers

cane of emerald pointing toward the brow
when the wound returns with its slugs
as if feeding on oil-cake without bovine desire
the crowns of our heads are enlarged extracting
without stopping the brain from the head
the migraine that stopped the medicine with its
preferred needles, the anvil blows, the bird-like peck!

Weep, man, beloved brother, ass, bending your back!
Learn how it was, will be tomorrow, coming from your
   desert
father-camel, how the oasis was sunk because of your hump
and, wandering, the bird that sings of yōur sixpence
calls the sixpence back, cat-like the lamp in your eyes
meditating on nothing, the raving dog
life, life!

The powder with which I'll perfume myself
has just arrived with its mirror that shattered
my profile before my profile was born!

Caliban

Mute, suspended from cliff to his grave
listening to demonic violins;
if he bellows the thorax expands in dialect
teeth gnawing at the spleen that stored up too much blood

stepping on that ancient secretion washed out to dry
if the allergic cough excels in alligator pepper
let it be brutal in lost tonsils, in the curve of his frenum
waiting on the sole of the tongue, the palette of the feet
over bent speech, illuminations of raw death
in the lustre of vampires
now that in reviewing his lot he descends
headlong into pain, operatic in green pepper
feeling in spasms of rage
how the umbilicus was raped by pestilential blood

but listening to this final nocturne
he will pause in death to wash his face
which is after all a stroke of good fortune
he will keep it under his arm, putting out Salvador Dali's
　donkey
collapsing in flames with his bruised hand
he will share his last bottle with us arguing over
the beast of his life, crying to stop him
from pulling out his hair, from disgracing
the never-was-life-so-difficult moment
organic suffering stitched to his collar
is all he takes with him, this clobber
this earth of antediluvian death which he understands!

Pilgrim

Eyeing the Milky Way we go on pilgrimage
getting tonsured to the bone to the root
suffering from mystic fever, surrendering
to those doubts that defy naming; timeless sensations
when we accompany our profiles to be born
leaning on silhouettes when we walk, then
putting on our masks at the moment of growing up
before going to the infinite point of being so tiny
being so startled when the drumroll calls us
flat on the silver, picking up those famous
thirty pieces of silver at the eclipse of speech
and finally these thrilling sensations of the cadavers
when we accompany our profiles to die.

Functioning ostrich they have told us to watch
when it curls its neck to see, how silent its solitary gaze
this bird which like man runs when it surprises itself
with its immense strength when it reduces itself
to kill the lice that lodged in its posterior
without compromising the numerical ancestor
in solitude, in its majesty, this timeless bird
of the awesome father; monastic ideas
articulate in fingers the speech of the damned
and each man becomes a hermit soliloquizing
in Arabic coffee, in English tea the thought
springing up like thorns through the adrenal gland
facing the last point of hope we reach out
for that hand dangling from the sky to be saved
by him O sea drawing from ocean to ocean the fibroid nerve

so that looking at the sun watching the stars
so that rising from the crucible of this life
dreaming of woman dreaming of Amon this road will be
   clear
this eye that bled its night of lachrymose blood
will smile its morning of Promethean sun
horseman of the imagined and the living hand
holding the fire set to the herb I smoke
because man was born tiny stretched out in his crib
chained to Adam before beginning the bitter pilgrimage of
   life.

Sonata and Rain

My father who was sheltered from rain
by those broad cocoa leaves over
long distances in the hurricane August
of successive years when the cold
whistled through the shattered begging
villages, my father with his lantern-glass
image, in whom two thoughts went racing
over mother while building a house for grandmother
when he was only the son of his father
dead in the memorable year of the son
becoming the father at sixteen

Father, sometimes I see how you came
over youthful boulders to the threshold
of man, in the infinite tenderness of woman
bearing the loneliness of those years
coming on tranquil Sundays to your organ
where you played sonatas while singing
into the distant night, your distant dream

the path of manhood we traverse, conscious
at each step of the fragile destiny of man
gift of life we take into that day
when moulding the earth we bake our bread
drink a glass of rum before the hour
for putting out our flame with our fate
but before we leave all behind, before each
gambler rolls his last dice
believe me Father, there are sons who

never having been born to be fathers
suffered the father locked inside the child
and likewise men who never having been the sons
tied round their waists the task of their fathers
moribund like your days now passing
through the meridian of my own life.

Illumination

Approaching middle age, the thirty-eight steps
upon forty, I think of my grandmother approaching
a century: so little her forgetfulness!
so beautiful her youth, so gentle her face!
My grandmother determined to outlive the century
having outlived her tragic grandchildren in the rot
of their lives, cries into her handkerchief their absence
retelling the grief of the young dying of their burdens
before covering the distance between them

day which resembles her number, the gifted queen
of miracle unperturbed by the reaches of science,
permitting only a toxic herb into the dry of the bones
to prolong the female of creation, could pass
without disturbing the peace of her face

my grandmother approaches a new cycle
and I know that if she has lived double my age
the margin between us speaks less about her past
and more about my number cut on the edge of a stone

My life scored on a discordant note so that I hear
only the faint sound of a timpani telling me
how to hope: I know the more I strive to get
to her age the more she distances herself from me
for while I approach painfully the threshold of forty
she lives on and on having survived better
than her grandchildren the ravages of life.

Bread

The spoon was walking, full, off the table
to reach the poor and all their Sundays,
all their lost mornings came rushing back
hungry as the lion's eyes; the table was moving
toward the centre, breaking its legs
and all their journeys came inward to their stomachs
reeking of this great forest's hunger
the loaf was walking out of the oven announcing
its magic yeast and the mouths of the poor
began to shake trying to catch the taste of its smoke

O bread that walked away from its smoke
only to deny that other smoke that sat
on the flat of the lip, begging for the broth
of the frog to warm the frost-bitten mouths
O soles so rich in holes from biting hard on the flesh
of the leather as if the journeys led somewhere
looking at these soles it would have been nice
to keep for once the grain that they produced
to bake their own bread it would have been nice
to drink for once the milk from their cow
before they confiscated it from them
be nice, sitting up all night, unable to breathe
because of that asthmatic seizure, to smoke a rare leaf
be nice not to have been the man I have been!
but who can choose one's own spoon
to eat at a round table to one's heart's desire
embroidered lace and all, the hearth at full glow
warming these rheumatic joints, a nice contemplation

of a beloved woman the song of Orpheus
eyeing at the end of the tunnel the mouth of the muse
calming this heart that sits on the palm of my desire
but having looked back and lost it all
when the spoon rolls off the table with its tomorrow
when the oven announces its fresh bread at a price
denied the multitude, denied my pocket I ask only
that when they hope for it begging on their knees
give them this bread, this universal gift!

The Baptism of the Orphan

Orphan when you are struck by your despair
walking on one foot only to get down to rub
your clubfoot with the oil of the eye; Orphan
to stroke the thighs of the beloved dreaming;
legs of the anguish, stroking between two ripe-firm breasts
the ripe sweetness of the beloved who curls
inside her sheet with the slyness of a cat;
solace when it is sweetened by desire, the calm look
on the face of the orphan after the wild storm
for the lips of his diamond so delicately shaped
so desperately desired only to wake up from his dreams
to see it going into the belly of the earth trembling
because the morning of hallucination had arrived
with its cloud of locusts its sea of prehistoric birds
and written all over the sky by the indelible marks
of their claws, written all over the world
by the russet-coloured wings of the female
was the tale of how the orphan lost his leg
searching for his imaginary diamond
that had long lost its brilliance
resting in the inpenetrable belly of the earth

So in this mist of uncertain morning you grieve
because you were baptised with the wrong name
with your eyes open with the look of the iguana
and the earth which kept your umbilical cord
had revolted because the knowledge of how you were born
the secret of how you came out legs first
had started the latent quarrel between God and man

and having no father or mother to sing of
on the banks of the river, at the border of the two roads
where all waifs retrieve their lost childhood
you go with trepidation mapping out the world
on the palm of your hand, searching for that other tale
stolen with its fire, the shameful baptism
of how the grief came to the sea looking
at the face of the orphan, how endlessly perturbed
by the mystery of looking at our mirrors at night
we hear the voices of the dead, the tremor of those
who having died before stroking the legs of their beloved
return, denying conception, without mother or father
with only the stone for a name!

To a Dead Poet

for Agostinho Neto

A journey separates us now
separates me from you implacably dead.
You have heard it said in life:
the purity of this life comes from the palatine desire
to die for one's belief, written in your blood
the diaphanous resolve for which the Zambesi broke its
    banks.
Should I recall you now, mourn you in verse, the leaves
of your *imbondeiro*[1] no longer green in my hands?
Antonio your sun went down that evening
tragically your sun of gold stolen from the poor
the white eagle's talons dripping blood from your heart
flying to the south where they hang men in black.

Etched in my memory you lived at the foot of an island
where neither guest nor enemy of Cabral the wide Atlantic
was the exile you shared with the *dugongs*[2] on the coast
writing the poems of revolt I recall with sadness:
the whip on the plantation, the black labourer
counting the hour, waiting for his woman's return
from the nightly service rendered to the overseer
all that tremulous rage, Antonio.
When their flutes were silenced by war
and the sons went away from their fathers
poet you raised from the ashes the phoenix
and women wove a burlap of joy round your name
you were their hope the light their dignity restored

the poetry that transformed slaves into men
and mistresses polluted by plantation blood
return hoping to be mothers once more
bearing the dark sons of your name.

---

¹*imbondeiro*   Large tree found in parts of Angola and Southern Africa.
²*dugongs*   Aquatic mammals with a fish-like body, flipper-like forelimbs and no hind limbs. Related to the manatee. A seacow.

The Brotherhood of Man

The locomotive breaks its run
you descend to adjust your gaze
your century, looking through your narrow point
back into the Australopithecus grove, where, starting,
we hurried to arrive, naïve pleadings, into the rush of age

pagan journey I could tell, when this heart
begins to beat, was no sooner contemplated
before these crevices in my face marked my time
for the poet is he who travels everlastingly
embracing his neighbour embracing his enemy
to love life more to hate death less
in the red evenings the taste of fate
already salting my wounds with regret

goodnight, let us say farewell before we cry
so that when the fireflies dance round our shadows
nothing would remain but this grove where we ate
the primeval meal before leaving the warm cluster of love
for this cold taste of fate, this glacial world
this night, the locomotive continuing its run
into the never-ending day when I shall embrace tearfully my
  enemy.

The Gambler

Mindless of death we plunge into the depths of desire
before the rite of spring, steal a curtain
from the sea whose mystery like the eye of the storm
is us returning from the belly of the whale
with only the plankton of this life.

Queen of Spades will the gambler escape
looking so satisfied, so greedy, holding the three cards
while I move this ace shoulder to shoulder
betting on my life, thinking of a drunken Yesenin?

Tense, waiting for sacred bread, we survive on
the stalk of the cereal over which we fought yesterday
torn like a terse idea punctured by two constantly
opposing claws expressed in the grizzly bear
of existence putting the jinx on our feet
walking for American nickel to kill off our torment

it is good that watching the vulture's flight
we shall arrive, uninvited, at the feast for the dead
good that following the hyena's track we shall
steal a rib from the sun-dried deer; good that before
they throw us out of this hotel room on our backs
we shall write a little poem in our blood
good that we live so short, good we die so long!

The Afternoon of Your Diamond

Furthermore, in spite of this ennui
little is achieved in life
beyond continuing the sin of Adam
raising a hand against your brother like Cain
furthermore, dazzled by this equinoctial storm
like the beginning of the fall of man
we go aimless into the desert
as when gravitating to the top of our horizon
to the top of each of our trees we stumble
on the rocks until a good Samaritan shall pass
touching our backs with the horn of a bull

and then, returning, saved,
staring at our former image sitting upright
at dawn? so much never to be that again!
so much never to trim our nails again, to clown for joy
before dusting out the mote in our eyes; thinking of
   benediction
the day is already dark with the equinox
nebulous streak of fate as when the wind passes
through my room, passes through your heart
no one shall hear how by the heart imploring
listening to Mahler we arrive at the gates of Jerusalem

so March, thirty-one at birth, grows
with its hard broom to sweep out this morning
the dark Saharan sky, disturbing the gems we lost
before squeezing our poppies, and all being well
you will ride on the back of a storm, holding your throat

flute player hearing yourself in the tenor of an afternoon
in the treble resonance of a fracture
sustained from descending to heights
playing for your crushed diamonds
in the terrible loneliness of a grave desire!

Children of Amnesty

The prisoners who march single file
to the sound of their chains
the women who weep comforting the children
of the departed men
    — already I hear the deathknell —
the orphanage swollen by the executioner's call
these men who march noble in their ancient belief
O profile in stone that lets your greatness be!
Primordial beings that started the world
with a great profundity of words;
great your essence like the force of a storm.

contemplating your death
does that frighten you now? Does that
in other words make your faces apocalypse of the end
so much blood sweated in the sun so much tenderness
   checked
and to write when I smell you in the waist of my symbol
when I hear you in the speech of the revolver
the monolith that runs crazed on the edge of the knife
and the initiates their false baptism for power!
Betrayed by them, do they recall the country
where they spoke in platitudes how they loved the poor?

I shall be consoled by your courage
acolytes of the offering the eagle ensnares you
into its world where the sad cadenza of life
shatters the silence of our age
I shall be consoled, because your blood transforms
our patch of dry earth
into a river of luminous dawn.

The Night of the Beasts

Seven feet by seven when the night
invades threateningly the walls of the cell
and the warden performs his monotonous habit of praying
before locking up his charge; seven feet sculptured in stone
set to perfection like that other six feet dug in the earth;
again they have imprisoned him, whipped him in profile
held him up, his heart beating, facing the brazier
so that thinking of his mother in the night of the beasts
the son of woman shakes convulsively
before covering his face to cry

burnt out in skeleton, this country's image
has a vicious look it resembles a dagger's edge
it speaks chapters of brutality of villages nakedly scarred
of rivers infested with corpses of graves hurriedly covered
this country whose heart has the beat of a river
amazed at the size of its own flood
whose history born out of the vertical rupture of the earth
no longer remembers the rape of its own pulsating female

prisoner of conscience, the man paces seven feet
by seven, resembling a deranged civet
the beasts have beaten out his brain, only his
nightmare is left flowing from a sea of dead urchins
a lava of bad blood gushing from the head of his country
and reliving it all over again he hears a tune like
death's larghetto into the dawn where his beloved
waits in tears holding a bouquet of flowers.

Prisoner of Conscience

The magistrate has freed me
from this cell which numbered six
into the year, in solitude, in faeces by the bucketful
during which they scarred my name in monogram at the foot
of my soul dying from being too much of my soul!

Blood rupture in the head when they came at night
was it there, suspended from the ceiling, that
beating the El Salvadorean man, the torturers
worked the pincers into the head of the Guatemalan
screaming like a beast for the ten thousand
'disappeared' names unmentioned by John Paul the Second
lighting a candle for the vortex of his Polish land

Twelve hammer blows to crush his skull, Steve Biko
was saying: numberless families are on the island,
during the reign of the laager
while when they hit me in the rest
of my Africa, when the rhinoceros draws blood
from their throats the women will confess to save their children
and Benigno Aquino's blood is shed to drive out a tyrant.

The magistrate has freed me
from this cell but the two thousand cells
of others open and close in the prison of my soul!

They Shot the Poet Once

Someone is drafting a bill to throw the wounded poet out
someone, an American Bantustan thinker, in the service
of **BOSS**, whose clamouring for the Brutus man unleashes
vertigos in the State Department while
the tennis player luxuriates on capitalist grass
after emasculating the Chinese sage.

Venus they will explore you into the raw
of the solar system they will uncover your inscrutable
cloud cover, they will penetrate your surface to feed
an insatiable hunger while the desires of the poor
of Chicago, the destitute in Detroit hardly touch
the planners who ship bullets and advisers
across the Rio Grande where the born-again Christian
general spreads the gospel like poison to the peasants

elbowing through this travesty a dog barks
in rage, a dog of mangy coat, who carries
in his flight the scabs of the poet's wound
so that petrified judges at the sight of this angry dog
shall re-think the fate of man, the better to absolve
their conscience, the better to sleep at night without
the nightmare about the poet's back dripping with blood
where they shot him once!

The Refugee

for Muin Beseisu

Orphaned memory returns to his head
it is calling, come from that place
where he lived so much of yesterday
orphaned memory through the aperture, in exile
when it hurts him with its sad tenderness
whispering it wants to be loved

but coming against this love, he sees
buried under the rubble, dripping with blood
ten thousand Palestinian children, ten thousand banished
 hopes
marked with the new swastiskas, orphaned memory
to remake the holocaust by those who survived it
churning the blood of children who already beggars
in the streets lose their limbs in the macabre dance
of a thousand eyes for an eye

he is waiting for him, waiting for his own Moses
to forget the frenzied yesterday, looking for the release
of the white dove of the Galilee rising from the ash
to flay the bad conscience of American silence
while grinning in Jerusalem he sits eating Polish sausages
made from the flanks of ten thousand little children
the new king of the holocaust!

The Children of Palestine

for Muin Beseisu

Pronounced animals by his rabbi in the cruel absence
of men; starved, cramped and suffocating in camps
having been condemned by the Torah in his hawk-like
apocalypse, he sends his tanks among children, to smother
creation, the butcher of Jerusalem!
so save for that child whose body reeks of blood
what has he left untouched after he invaded Sidon
save for that old man blinded by cluster bombs
what has he gained after bombing the hospital
while the Litani flows, flows with the corpses
of Palestinians and the guilt of the world

do they no longer carry the scars, these vengeful tribes?
see how they converge to kill now, see how they move
in the labyrinth of hate, Saracens crawling, crawling
with a brutal desire to destroy fanning the flames
of this crop of hate blazing in the desert!
now building his Sparta the general observes
his procession of slaves bowing under the Jewish whip
he laughs amidst the ruins of Sidon, he guffaws amidst
the dead of Damur, he dances relishing his kill
the general bemedalled by his king who drinks
his wine from the skull of a child unearthed by his tank

great ideas are floating now: they died these parasites
to defend our borders, they died these children to protect
our own, their eyes punctured with a thousand splinters
naked putrefaction of hate disdaining God and man while
   the *dinar*[1]
grows capital in trade, while the Torah recites the credo:
they died being neither brother of the Jewish lobby
nor favoured relation of the Arab swimming in oil!

---

[1] *dinar*   A unit of currency found mostly in the Arab world.

Aftermath

These are the ruins the burnt-out bodies
which no riot of the Mediterranean can efface
these are the ruins: a child walking armless into the night
searching for her mother's face, a man digging through the
  rubble
hoping to recover his last son's corpse, these are the ruins
with which we write a blood-stained page into the history
of Beirut! a child's skull is not a cup a woman's torso
is not a ball, a refugee camp is not a battlefield
but these are the ruins they fill my nights with
colour my days with so that no memory of 1939, no
  mention
of their Jehovah can efface this crime

A stump! a cripple! when the innocent feels
the assassin's boots! is this how they reshape
a destiny bedevilled like an orphan's rage
the spiral hawk of death which nightly steals
from the beleaguered souls the last vestiges of love

sometimes the desert throbs with a million muted cries
and men the better to scorn a God gone silent but awake
trample in the dust the yearnings of a generation
but they await the next passover they who no longer pray
having neither sons nor rams for the burnt-offering.

The Tin Gods

Watching the tombs tonight
the desert raises its shadow the desert
sees the caravan along its own arm:
playing this game of words the desert fights
over each word the sound of the noun
the ink on the scribe's page forgetting
the trail taken by the twin mules;
the desert's path is like two vessels
from a fountain consecrated by God
because the man who cried at the wailing wall
is brother of the man driven out of Palestine

prelude to an oasis of blood, I write
these lines against the book they quote
to silence the voice from the minaret
I write thinking of those who say at daggers drawn
to talk to the diplomats gives fresh baptism
to the music of Wagner

blood flows from the Litani
blood flows in Elait, in Sidon
where the white dove is strangled in its flight
and where the wandering Bedouin in search of his brother
the Jew is corralled because already the tin gods
drink the blood of the vineyard before the ripe harvest!

The Zealots[1]

This evidence here penetrates my skin
grafting a toxic film into my bones
which are my bones clashing against their joints
and the equidistant love grows fiery leaves
seeking a reluctant sun to warm this variegated tree
on which they hang a mutilated sign

watchful Lord we rummage through this chaos
before the descent of the vultures to tear out
their remains, looking for telltale signs in their hearts
where they profaned the liturgy of the prophet
in this carnage emasculating God!

and the severally misquoted book: abused,
smeared; what priest thrown to the ground
without the power of the invisible rod
permits these sharks, these false teachers
to disembowel those who called them frauds
before plucking out their eyes making larger
the darkness already shrouding their souls

when they have washed their hands in the blood of this
   carnage
the desert'll hide its own shame in its blood, the desert
already fattened by the caravans passing through its heart
bearing merchants all golden-robed chanting the litany
for the commerce they so desperately wish returning
from the pilgrimage while the desert prophesies
a season of monstrous deeds!

---

[1]*The Zealots*   In October 1982, Moslem fanatics went on the rampage in the northern Nigerian cities of Maiduguri, Kano and Kaduna, killing and mutilating hundreds of people.

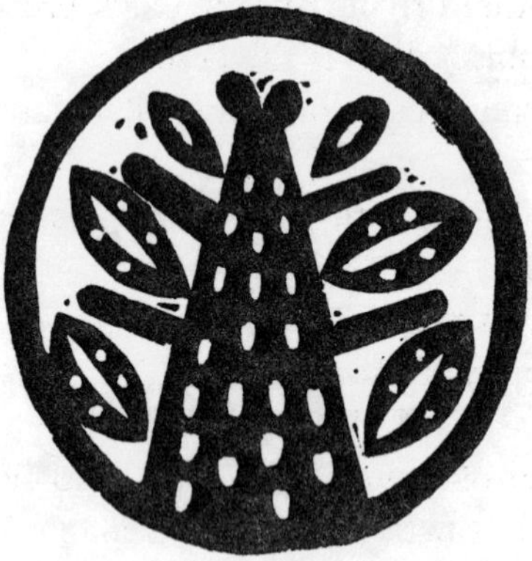

Exodus

Everything echoes of the past:
the chains of the slave, the march of the Jew
the fleeing of the Palestinian; these inhuman acts
of tin gods outdoing each other to preside
over the demise of man; now they have added
to their list the wretched of the earth!
The black brother driving out the black brother
all along the coast, all over the desert
they go, these bundles of rags, the Ghanaians and the
 Tuaregs
the beggars of Niger with their skeletal bones
into the desert
where death awaits
them at the appointed time.

O men so short of memory O darkness so clever
to shroud the instinctive goodness in man
quick of the sword, the demagogues employed
to whip up this horror, this curse on my people;
to what barbaric priest we owe this revelation
this beating of their breasts to justify the crime?
Aghast the world is watching illiterate minions
and eunuch politicians digging up the grave of ghosts;
ten times over I shall repeat:
we live for a while with our gold and conceit
but die painfully among the stones paying for the crimes
we fill the history of man with century to century!

Song on a Chinese Flute

Forgetful of season the desert raises a storm
forgetful of traveller the oasis lowers its waterline
and the desert hears its own cry in the bark of a wild dog
the howl of a hyena; patient Lord arrest this day!

Stampeded by camels this desert's pulse measures high
on the Richter scale its belly resembles a toxic waste
so that staggering the traveller follows the tracks
of an *addax*[1] to a waterhole already stinking of death

and if through this desert's lenses we see the world:
the slaughtered in Assam, death's leaping flames
over the heart of Central America; if this desert
becomes the heart of Zimbabwe whose wounds already
   sutured
they prick open once again, then what after this arithmetic
we say to the shy *jerboa*[2] completely disgusted with man?

Poets, we despair of ever finding peace, of holding
the cup of hope to the lips of mankind, and sitting
in my house tonight facing the desert, the air reeks
of human blood for they have murdered God and man
but I am consoled by him, who brings me
the wayfarer's songs, the shepherd on a Chinese flute

earth has no finer vision of peace than Mahler's
eternal sound; I bow to the master who has given me peace
in spite of the ME who despairs at every news of my
   WORLD.

---

¹*addax*   A large pale-coloured antelope of North Africa.
²*jerboa*   A mouse-like rodent found in North and, some dry parts of,
West Africa.

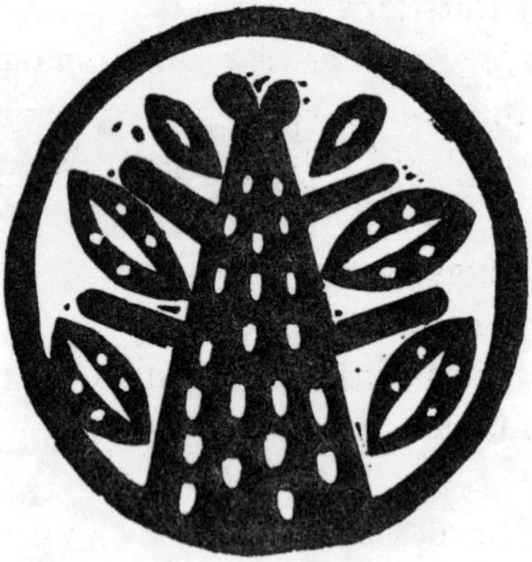

The Masquerade

Call the rainmaker back, this day's terror
reigns too long over the heart of the desert
deforming the camel's hump which stores eternally
the mythical water until this latitudinal point
throws up its season of skeletal gift

rainmaker, my thirst, my desert!
The masquerade year after year, until raving
they seek out the stone caves to read once again in
the ancient hieroglyphics the destiny mapped out for them.

The morning hangs over our lives
a cliff-hanger hides all the cards
the dramatist reveals little until finally he surprises us
with an ace to flatten our resolve

the wandering hordes, when will they return
with the same old scabs, the same old grunts
a masquerade to beg more aid?
tragically the old habits die hard
this Sahel rates high on the warped conscience
of some while the comprador class poisons the water-holes
to reap large capital abroad after compromising the
    rainmakers.

Stone

But one day the hot belly of this desert
which stretches at every movement of the sun
and one day this life seemingly endless in its woes:
a dog eating her pups, a suicide slashing his wrists
all this mess before we come to the grave of our illusion
will end, the belly drowning its victims in its blood

the cardiologist gives me permission so I smoke
a Turkish tobacco, tormented by these fireflies
in my head; wandering, I have scraped the bark
off the trees, scorched the earth and beaten my chest
I have played a dangerous game or two with my cards
my shadow and I but still found no answer

now I have come to love the beaten flesh
of stones, eaten the poisonous heads of puff-adders
listened to the song of certain winds bearing
no message of a life redeemed from falling on the cold flesh
of these stones avoiding the epileptic man flat on his face
and I go, leaning on my cane, to retrieve joy
imprisoned in the watery eyes of a wounded dog.

Solstice

Is this dog's wound like my own
Like the flaming heart of the desert lacerated
by the breath of the sun, preparing for the millennium
when the men already compromised by the state remember
in order that they might regret, diabolical sun,
how the dinosaur in spite of its size
had the laggard brain of the jack-ass

the desert's journey is long, the desert remembers
the summer solstice when shaded by the ancient *baobab*[1]
I sat, eating dried dates, thinking of Perseus:
to kill with one hand their Medusa to flatten
with one blow the judge of the inquisition
so that on redemptive Tuesday men shall be men
Tuesday when they receive pagan baptism

the cross which fails for being no more his church
the wine which discolours its bottle
when you see the blood in the dog's eyes
learn how crossing this desert in search of a cure
we begin again the destiny of man
leaving the shelter of the ancient *baobab*

the oasis already has the water to calm my heart.

---

[1] *baobab*   Very large tree found all over West Africa, but mostly in Sahel region. Produces a delicious, gourd-like fruit favoured by monkeys.

Logos

The turtle comes grumpily to predict Armageddon
and the chairs in the house where I live
begin to recede into a corner where I buried my childhood
if I stammered this moment would pass
in spite of this lingering spasm in my head
provoking a cry down to the root of the *alveolus*[1]

remorseless day I am too tired
to look through this looking-glass
at this triangular gift baited by the sun
content to keep on scratching my wounds
until I peel off ligaments of my regret
bandaging for later a patch of good fortune I stole from
   Aurora

turn the tide Aurora let the stream flow south
in this season ravaged by thunderstorms
dawn the world with your brilliance
the sun is breaking let the seaweeds grow
the algae was sad which saw me dreaming
facing the sea for the locks of a mermaid's hair

a medley of crickets and fauns
beneath my window, castanets and rings
summoning the dead to the dance;
when the new Pied Piper plays who shall follow
into that day when the colours of the rainbow
like a peacock's tail merely move a heart inchoate
into a morning lucid with hope?

---

[1] *alveolus* A little cavity, pit, or cell; an air cell in the lungs; (here, a socket within the jawbone).

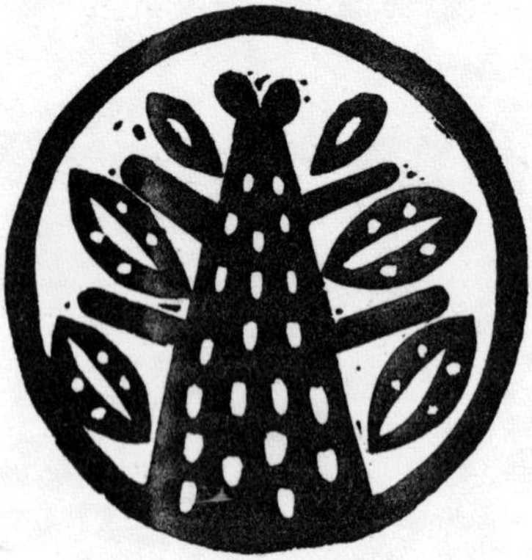

Rite of Passage

This melody hurts; for whom is it played
when to dance, as usual, opens the veins
of our bruised memories to the needle's prick
O strange melody, O excruciating night!

October and dancing in the heat but don't stop now
preparing for the next feasting the coming of Artemis;
don't go blindly like an elephant into the forest
uprooting the trees, destroying the foliage in your rage
and don't blot out your memories of blood-curdling seasons
when, liberated, we may not know with which hand to hold
this precious bark, eat this mysterious fruit saved for us

the melody is playing and you embrace the dark
it is all you have, this stupefying sound of music
like a pagan rite of passage, intoxicating, barbarous
renewing our desire to eat from the same bowl the
   uncooked meal
to purify our souls, stirring up our resolve
when we move on to the next stage, where, levitating
we shake off the fear of being cowed
by the demons who wished us quiet, who plotted our
   deaths.

Song

*'Ninety-five percent
of my people poor'*

Edward Brathwaithe

On those islands where they changed their names
they go back to their roots, mounting the last block
where they were sold, where they were baptised in pain
the sea acting as reluctant priest; these nameless shells
broken upon the shores, these plaintive cries of islands
spread across the face of the Atlantic;
I hear this song of shanties of castaways bracing up
for the storm hear this wailing of a past that begs
for redemption from Caliban's chain to give new rhythm to
   roots!

The past which echoes of bitter memories sends them
in search of that leaf so as to forget what the history
books tell so as to form that brotherhood that dulls
the pain of cupping their hands to drink the bitter bark
of their sweat bought for the price of a brochure telling
the world of white sand of artifacts so grotesquely comical
in the shops denying the rebellious song of their misery
woven into their dreadlocks of desire

play the song, debased brother! the dogs of hunger
howl in your head; the old god is dead, the emperor
who knew the ancient word, the Babylonian sorcery
but when you take your song from island to island

telling of regenerative man, when the tourist board
no longer announces your passivity and rum-soaked fever
give us a new song, the age of Shango; for no longer victims
of Sisyphus you hurl thunderbolts to the sky
revealing the lark soaring with your expectation.

The Soldier

He is wearing his hat he is wearing his moustache
like a waxed medallion, today he is wearing the silence
that crept into his head never having spoken to the sun;
crepuscular world where reduced to nameless toys
in the game of war we smoke the opium from the golden
  triangle
what have you done to his youthful dreams
in what sad bedrooms did he bargain for his sanity
in a language riddled with exploitation and contempt

dying slowly today this is all he remembers:
a polyglot of rehearsed phrases the smell of geraniums
lavender bosoms weary of pleasing youths lost
in the mists of battles, and perhaps a child abandoned
to please his mother and the girl waiting back home;
but at night between sadness and insanity
like two seas apart, he breaks down, wanting to be once
  more
the son over whom his mother kept watch

stray dogs we all are, passing through the camel's eye
possessed perhaps by the indescribable madness
that is opium for success until like rotten fruits
we are heaped on top of each other in madhouses
where only the rattle of our teeth, the reflex of our arms
reaffirm our last link with the human fold
the dying need to be forgiven and understood
in our sorrow, having served better the delusion of men
than listening to the cries of the just, the maimed!

The Artist

Portraits drawn to reveal his world
I know it, cut to his form, seeking
what answer swallowing that drug?
portraits I tell myself, recalling him
cutting off an ear, having in sum his humanity
thinking about which I have called him back
from the grave to see better these portraits
meditating on his hurt, feeling how he reached
from earth to sky his stained-glass blue
his reason wrenched from his head

he strained, his obelisk, to reach his credo
how fecund his world, how despite himself
he looked into his soul, the blue of reason, the yellow
of seeing that which was written in the moon's face
his journey toward the infinite, grave ideas
that pull man out of the roots of his hair
and then contemplating his torment shut him out

in a garden alive with sunflowers are patterns
of life, patterns of death sketched in blue

Kyrie eleison, his life, his stained-glass blue!

Childhood

So late in my life, some things I have remembered:

In the morning I did not wash my face upwards
the trickster had more cards than I dared admit
for him to trick me so, and my childhood uncannily
comes back to me in hiccups

stammering my good morning two words apart
my mother teaches me to speak, watching over
the fall of my stuttered words, the half of my alphabet
swallowed in rage before it was born, being
that I was born the son of my stammering father

my mother trying to loosen my tongue gives me
water out of a bell and the chickens in our yard
scratch, scratch away at my meal to free the grain
of my resolve; my mother speaking on my behalf

and my left-handedness which set my mother thinking:
a cat is a thief, the left-handed child has a similar fate
my mother holding my left hand behind my back so that
I will write with my right hand, to be the right son

so late in my life, some things I have remembered:

how they tampered with my brain, the left-sided thought
the right-sided sadness, how endlessly I go the child
of an image in a world that died long, long ago
how my ravaging desert started to spread in my childhood!

The Muse

Drifting in mid-stream we cling
to a fragile reed hoping for calmer seas
and the poem always an elusive lover
becomes a baptismal rite.
Mary Magdalene you weep so much for him
let us consecrate unvirgined woman!

Comet you hide so cleverly from the sea
letting the original mother despair
but the child wished by her heart
arrives to suck the breasts of woman
it etiolates desires murmured in darkness
O noble creation!

Always this labour to be born
and the poet remembers the first baptismal drink
brewed from the toxic herbs
they brewed it stronger than the vinegar offered him
he who was released at noon
while the poet's cloak is eternally worn

woman you say so much in ferns
your hands dissolve into waves
and when I float on the tide of longing
you touch me with your comb
the sea embraces me in the night
and I wait for the dawn to fish for your spoon
but you dawn in the song of Daphne
woman that I compose
every day the sea embraces me in your waves

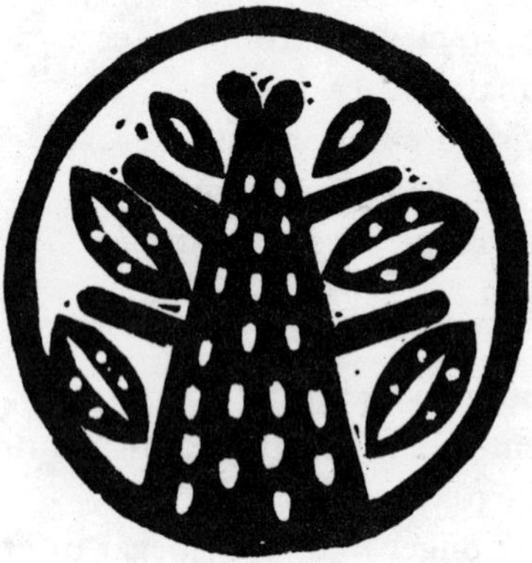

Anniversary

Grafted upon my heart I embrace him
ten years always and say: man you talk
in my sleep, the night smells of formaldehyde

grave of my remembrance
if you rise, if you move, slab of the revolving years
cement which upturns cement, stone which is stone,
who shall come to witness this flame, this night
of carnal passion the grave has for the body
the figure which rises when my memory brightens
tragically its thoughtfulness

let this dirge be brief!
I might relive again the season when reading
astral signs my card began to move to my heart
and my temples already numbed from grief
my heart already frozen at the thought of him
woke to the beating of a violent day

who has eaten my bread
who hovering like a hawk has stolen
the chicken I bought for today
who reminds me to remember
who when it rains reads in my face how my heart
rained torrentially night after night ten years into a grave?

The Sun

The needle touches the centigrade high
I move back into the shade
letting the hearse pass
afraid of boiling afternoons

Obsessed? No! but I prefer the day
which amputates the limb of hunger
acknowledging the blood in the dog's eyes
so that strengthening it on calories
the dog shall repeat those evergreen desires
to gnaw at the lice on its back
in spite of the ointment we applied there
suspecting vegetable death

running I contemplate the time when I cease to be born
when growing I put behind me the image of the man
who hobbles on stick for his grain of rice
to buckle his muscles against his fiery evening
the dog's eyes are running blood they say in Sierra Leone
why blame the sun?
why deny the purity of that blood that greets me in every
    smile
blood which passes under the bridges evenings when I weep
    over
our destiny the hearse passing through the country of my
    soul!

Portrait

The multitude demanded:
send us the compradors, the crowd demanded:
send us, naked, the pirates so that we can witness
the miracle of oil oozing out of human greed
the lepers demanded: send us, without favour,
the fingers of the men bedecked with rings
so that we can smelt them to rejoice at the play of muscles
the miners exclaimed: send us for a day the diamond dealer
so that he can hear the sound of human flesh sizzling in the
  heat
the child shrieked: send me in tatters the man reduced
to a clown on the trapeze for shooting my father in jail
the beggars, furious, demanded loudly: send us crawling
on all four the merchants for having raised the price
of grain over our misfortune; the women shouted:
send us the cops who clobbered our children
for questioning the senators who stole our land
after promising us running water for our village
finally the multitude shouted loudly: we shall wait
no more, the honeymoon is over!

Night Whistle

The informers set me up in smoke
testing my courage, and my beard hides
a grin that scorns their two-faced regard
it contemplates laughter more poisonous
than the bite of puff-adders
for the heads of the soft-bellied fools
more cornered than the vanishing crocodiles

do they want my soul, these men?
The photographer takes pictures of my face
capturing each sigh, each fall of a frown
noting my unruffled journey that disturbs their sleep
while the wire-tapper plants microphones in my flowers
to record the poem I recite to the burrowing worms

let these jackals talk, the world is full
of barking mongrels, the faithful dog knows well
the ingratitude of the saved master
but if they desire my hide drying in the sun
if they contemplate me on green pepper
they have never looked into my eyes
which fix them with disgust
each morning I come down in laughter!

Mask

Holding the necks of their bottles
they are keeping a wake over my soul

when the grass was lean on this side of our world
who watered my thirsty desert who heard the harsh cry
of my throat, living so precariously on thorns?
The poet's task is done,
and all daggers yesterday pointed at him
all desires to drown him in his blood are dulled

a lone flute player plays a final refrain
for my soul; there is already enough earth
on it to forgo the final rite
as mourners already impatient with me
yearn for the religiose wine
and that bird, that bird that carried in its beak
a blade of grass taken from my heart
prepares a nest the pillow of my worth

bird, if you fly tomorrow
sing how my soul was pecked, how endlessly
I sang from cradle to coffin
for man whose face has the look of an eternal grave!

The Miracle of the Morning

Tomorrow morning at this time
recovering from the shock of his stroke;
Walt Whitman wrote about such a man
in his song for himself, now that I remember
as he demands, without getting it, a mirror
to see the reverse of creation, the face
which fled from its owner after loving him
rising from the vascular ducts

a touch of voodoo they suspect, a woman
or two combined with a secret implanted
in his balls felled that man from shoulder
felled him from his presumptions from his narrow breast
forcing him to look with awe at those who helped him up
those who lit the burnt offering before priest and scallywag

tomorrow morning at this time, learning
to touch once again the soft belly of the soil
adjusting to the touch of the creator;
what a great job the painter has done!
how without studying his profile he has captured
the face of the victim, and how tearing off
the mask of immortality the scorned man learns to live
now horrified at his own littleness
    – the absent yesterday!

The Walk of the Blind

They range in ages from eight to twelve
forming an arm-chain without the gift of dogs;
darkness, the out-stretched feet to what accepted fate?
They pick their way through the street as if walking
on minefield as if approaching a treacherous path
they whose eyes have been eaten by the desert's sand
they whose world has been drowned in polluted streams
the bitter diseases of fate, O painful youth!

But if these victims of our neglect should moan
if these abandoned promises reared their ugly heads
to demand, a knife to our throats, the justice for
failing to be our brothers' keepers, of having poisoned
the sun to deprive them of seeing, without begging,
the face of the false brothers profusely gifted with speech
if they lost their blindness, what price their revenge?

O destiny! O fate! O march of the waifs!
without itinerary without seeking to map out the world;
a slice of the graft collected by parvenus
could have stopped this grief, shaming the beasts
but they have already toughened their hearts these lotus-
   eaters
they fear no plague and having no nightmare in their sleep
they have abandoned the blind seers, tossing out pennies
to assuage their guilt while unctuous they speed off
shielding their faces from the picture of the walk of the
   blind.

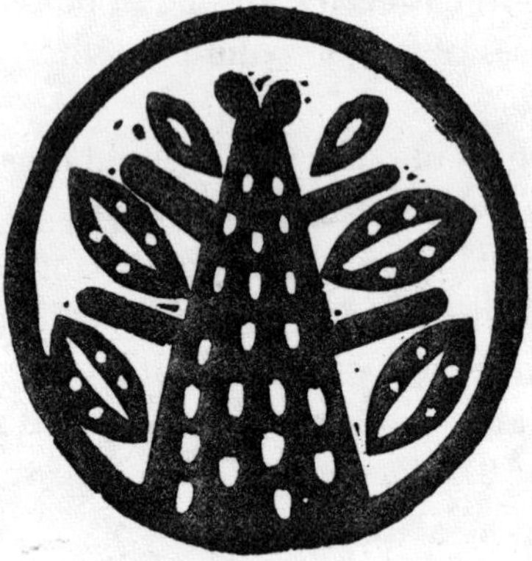

Desire

So you desire something better than this?
Something better than the monk's cowl
something better than the widow's mite
you desire, perhaps a chaise pulled
by a white horse, a coat of leopard skin;
a connoisseur of wine, you desire, no less
your own vineyard, a house on the Atlantic
you desire for posterity a mausoleum of gold
you desire finally all desires leaving no desire free

but if you rise from beyond that world
don't be surprised if through the obsidian morning,
no longer mesmerised, is DESIRE walking, all skeletal
but fuming; don't be surprised if struggling to speak
though his wish is misunderstood,
is the leprechaun the half-brother of man;
for all things desire a DESIRE:
the animal its lair, the fever its medicine
the one-footed man his two-footed walk
the blind man his morning of bright sun
the termite its corpse, the soil its guano
but to desire all, aye, to desire the face of the moon itself
perhaps I hear the waves saying makes the sea lecherous
with its own desire to eat up this filth
this world, this handiwork of man!

Dead Eyes

In the tavern where I slept last night
I went there to forget my bad luck
of a country sinking into neglect

now I am awake, and pulling up my pants
from desire, I say I cannot go back
I have lived so little on remembrance
lived so little on rain, knowing
I have lived so little on my country!

And it is enough that they do not know how it hurts
that in the blue waters of the country they have poisoned
the gentle *dugongs*[1] with the toxic power of their greed
but what can they preserve of that country for me
now that the desire to be man among the scorpions keeps
    me awake
thinking about the tattered history books
the desert which has eaten the heart of the savannah

so that every day Freetown is treacherously poised
above the bay where the capsized canoes
have the hang-dog look of a humanity that has died
Freetown from where they every day sail on their uncertain
    course
as if God had cursed this country shaped like a heart
but without the beauty of a peaceful heart

In the last flicker of your light
let me see the men who are lining
up
to cut up your heart.

---

[1] *dugongs* Aquatic mammals with a fish-like body, flipper-like forelimbs and no hind limbs. Related to the manatee. A seacow.

The Plague

Now to stop this desert encroaching upon my heart!

my Africa already diseased with its ubiquitous parasites
comes down with a fever and when the hurricane breaks
through the fragile veins of its body we glare at its ribs
the banana-riped putrefaction of its life

like cattle dying of *rinderpest*[1]
the men who are dying of gangrene
the women who drink a bucketful of water
and wake up the next morning surprised at their river-
    blindness
and the heart of this continent pulsates at every attack
by its wolves, its womb where the blazing furnaces of the
    droughts
make a bonfire of the carcasses of dead dreams
my Africa so long betrayed!

there is that part of her expanding tumour
that calls itself the giant of Africa
whose brain has fallen asleep
in whom the lizards burrow into their holes
to escape the rotten smell of decay
when the galloping pestilences of our world
are magnified and where a cynical philosopher
teaches his disciples to say DOOM instead of BOOM

We play a deadly game!
the dethroned monarchs wait in the shadows
to unfurl their magic carpets once again
but these brothers who speak the language of the hour
what malady has eaten their brains
that they suck ruthlessly the breasts of a continent
shrivelling like the leaves of the *oleander*[2]
in the relentless heat of our desert?

yesterday, I could have played the soothsayer
but who listens to Artemidoros these days?
There are already too many like him congesting our prisons.

---

[1]*rinderpest* An acute, usually fatal, virus disease of animals such as cattle or sheep.
[2]*oleander* A poisonous evergreen shrub or tree with fragrant white, pink or purple flowers.

Children of Adam

Trembling you surprised the snake
changing its skin; bald morning, transparent hunger
trembling you watched stretched-out age giving birth
to the next millennium, but it is no camouflage
this miracle, this commotion of colours
the skin not yet accustomed to its razor
not having crawled the length of an eye
to mirror its victims, unsuspecting
that the fangs withdrawn from speaking in ivory
false syllable, speaking in mimicry,
seek the eggs buried to hatch in the sand

and it will ovulate, slimy trickster, releasing
its own eggs it will ovulate when the unfortunate tortoise
leaves for a moment the hole where she buried her eggs
and if the clouds weep from seeing this crime
this mixing of eggs, if the earth shakes from shoulder
seismic agony, small matter if when we arrive
after the tidal wave to steal from the tortoise
her sacred gift, her rare telluric shells
we pick the eggs of the snake which, children
of Adam, we eat at once

for thus did death come into the world
all brilliant, paleolithic animal of cunning
who grows fat on our deceit; thus this tantalising
game of unearthing the diamond backs! thus we change
our names twisting the alphabets to steal the last eggs
but when she picks us up two by two laughing

when the parabolical eggs become the ubiquitous lie
in what glittering eyes we read how the tricksters
among us, changing their skins, paw us every day
bone to bone our skeletons the length of our lives?

This Side of Humanity

This morning is weeping facing my future
that collapsed surprised by its immensity
it imagines its own desire growing to monstrosity
thinking it's too late to begin, propitiously,
to change my destiny from falling grave on its knees
seeing that this enormous growth in my throat
was already killing me without watching
the cripple crawling across the street holding one leg
on top of his head disproportionate to his body

so I say so much for being that man
without having frightened with a knife the doctor
who invented the wheelchair, so much for seeing
him this side of humanity without the infinite desire
to unlock his legs from the snare on the pavement
I want to touch that man without insulting him
without forgetting the leper who comes
daily to the market with only a hole for a face!

elsewhere the year of the cock has ended
and they will fatten the pig, then puncture its belly
to offer to all comers the ripe blood of spring
but here where he falls, betrayed by his body
no one shall sit him straight, this man with his muscles
padlocked a fly hovering over his bowl
no one shall read in his eyes the pain of wanting
to be a father without ever holding a woman
without having looked into a cot wishing
to sing the song of childhood while a mother

watches the way his mother watched his cot
so today while giving him his meal I know
that he cries for all lepers behind that face
so beautifully ugly so terrifying to the child
who sells him bread, and having nowhere to go
I would like to invite him home
without scaring the women, without insulting
the judge, without having to explain
to the guardians of morality, the priests of tradition
how I love him, how he reminds me of the destiny
we all are travelling to without a guide!

the Game

...ncture, alone, oblivious of time
except for the metronome in your head
telling you the hour to rise the hour to fall
you exist contemplating the year, savouring your triumphs
which are only your defeats in the cloth of the sheep
for though counting only fourteen to its terminal cancer
of the year, December still keeps its surprises
those electric shocks that ruin in one volt
the face of the son of man

three hundred and sixty five rolled
into one; and we shall throw out in the end
the old stock, sweep out the old dust, wipe the mud
stuck to our boots, the old wife's tale, tossing
out the broom, all the accumulated letters
no longer guaranteed to ingratiate us
three hundred and sixty five in the poxy eyes of hope
and our resolutions broken before they were made;
a fanfare, goodbye, the year is ending
and we shall welcome the fine bridal mornings
they make such lovely promises these maidens
three hundred and sixty five to go before
forgetful of vows they sentence us, in spite
of those three wise men bringing gifts to the cradle,
to read the stars once again
December so profligate in HEART-QUAKES!
celebrate the birth! there is enough room
in this Christianity for all of us; so much
for picking up the symbol, so much for piling up

these gifts labelled the joy of Christmas!
but if counting three hundred and sixty five
you drain your soup bowl in a destitute's house
pick out the lice in your bread
if, *Minamata woman*,[1] you call on the Buddha
to drive out the bad omen, the night-owl of death
hovering over your beloved mercury-ravaged child
then let us share these gifts, the year is ending
goodbye this dragon-tooth, good morning
this scarlet pimpernel who comes to see
the blood in the desert's eyes!

---

[1] *Minamata woman*   Term derived from the sight of a Japanese woman in the town of Minamata. She was featured in *Newsweek* magazine in the late 1970s, holding her mercury-ravaged child in her arms.